REVENANT

POEMS

JACK B. BEDELL

BLUE HORSE PRESS REDONDO BEACH, CALIFORNIA   2016

REVENANT

JACK B. BEDELL

Blue Horse Press
P.O. Box 7000 - 760
Redondo Beach,
California   90277

Cover art: "Late Spring on Galway Quay"
by Jeffrey C. Alfier (2014)

Editors: Jeffrey and Tobi Alfier
Blue Horse Press logo: Amy Lynn Hayes (1997)

Epigraph from Harry Crews used by permission
of UNC-TV

ISBN 978-0692720639

ACKNOWLEDGMENTS

Special thanks to the editors of the publications in which these poems originally appeared.

"Raconte" (as "Old Story"), *5x5*

"Acutance," *Gnarled Oak*

"Coda" and "Les Ris," *Hoot*

"Morning, Vigil" *Southern Quarterly*

"Dead Turtle," *The Swamp*

"The Argument from Patience" and "Revenant," *Town Creek Poetry*

"Souvenir du Printemps," *Windhover: A Journal of Christian Literature*

"Coastal, Aberration" is based on a photograph, "Late Spring on Galway Quay," by Jeffrey C. Alfier, and after Joan Kane.

For My Family, Always

With special thanks to Marley and Kimberly Stuart, Richard Louth, and all the writers of the New Orleans Writing Marathon for their inspiration and example.

Table of Contents

Truth of the matter was, stories were everything and everything was stories. Everybody told stories. It was a way of saying who they were in the world, it was their understanding of themselves. It was letting themselves know how they believe the world worked the right way, and the way that was not so right.

— Harry Crews, from *The Rough South of Harry Crews*

The Argument from Patience

The stillness of the lake when a dos-gris dives
spreads in all directions. The water's surface
        flattens into pure reflection, sky

stretches away from the tops of trees,
herons tuck their beaks underwing, and I wait.
        I scan from reeds to horizon,

and wait. I hold my breath, squint
into the setting light for anything
        to break into the air, with nothing

to do but wait. I know the bird's not gone.
It's just not here. I know it will come back
        when its belly fills, maybe thirty yards

down the bank, but still here. This place
will find movement again. All waiting
        must come to an end.

Parabolic

His first summer married, my father tended
chickens. His job was to chase the birds
out of the tin coop on hot days. They piled
on top each other in the corner of the shed
no matter how hot it got in there.

He had to fight his way through their bodies
until he reached the back wall. Unless
he could tease the deepest chickens in the coop
to shuffle back out into the sunlight,
none of the other birds would leave.

Whenever he grabbed the ones pressed against the wall
and threw them towards the door, they'd run
back to press themselves into the flock again.
The only way to save the birds was to make them
choose the outside air for themselves.

If he couldn't, the whole dirt floor would be piled
white with dead feathers, too many bodies even
for the workers to carry home to their wives for supper.

Acutance

Pull in the nets,
swollen from seven passes off the Gulf.

White boots squeak on wet deck,
knots loosen and shrimp slide
out of twine, onto wood.

What rolled underfoot
now buzzes with shell and fin.

Sorting bins fill with overs and unders.
Lemon fish are swept into the hold for bait.

Stingrays flop to the sides
and are shoveled over,
reminders that days could be worse.

Dark Current

Stranded in our yard
    by backwash of river
        and a foot of rain,

a snapping turtle rolls
    on its shell, perpetual
        as if fallen in a dream.

Its claws cannot find river bottom
    for purchase, and nothing
        in the sea foam of leaves

gathering around its body
    can satisfy its chomping jaws.
        No wind to carry it

where it must go, no light
    bright enough to dry this mess,
        no brother, this storm.

Frissons

Sometimes a *yawp* comes
        from the marsh.

It echoes over the trees
        and stirs

turtles from their posts
        atop cypress logs.

Do not look for a bruise
        in the sky

or some vacuum of light
        sucking from that direction.

The hair will rise
        a certain way

on the back of your neck
        and forearms.

Follow these omens
        like compass needles

leading you some other,
        any other, place.

Revenant

On the Pass at Manchac
a camp has toppled from its pilings.
Its porch frowns down into the lake.

My son studies weather patterns
for class. His book claims
the wind circulating around us
is the same wind that stirred the sand
around Giza while men were building
pyramids, that swayed the lilies
of the valley and filled sails toward Vinland.

I imagine God sighing into clay
to give it life. Years later that breath
swirls into a storm off Africa,
dances for weeks across the Atlantic
into the Gulf and onto our shore
to nudge a camp off its perch
on the Point, the one place
my mother loved on her drive
back home, always rolling her window down

to feel a breeze in her hair.

Souvenir du Printemps

On his way to work, the father leaves his son
at the levee to count the persistence of woodpeckers
knocking in the tops of pine trees.

                                    The father's day
fills with well pressures, fishing tools,
men who cannot find wet in the rain.
The son's with snakes at the water's edge
and sugar cane to chew.

                                    Welders' dogs
scurry through the days of both, barking
where there should be quiet, quiet when
the men step outside for smokes.

                                    Field mice
wait inside the reeds for the sun to drop,
the father for all his pipe to come out of the ground
fully sound and ready for tomorrow,

                                    the boy
for supper when chairs fill and all hands join
in prayer, a meal set out for the taking.

Morning, Vigil

My uncle knew nothing still
wants to be moved.
He'd captained boats most of his life,

learned this pushing barges
around the intracoastal canal
by moonlight. It's why

he'd walk five blocks to St. Bernadette
in total darkness to wake the priests
for weekday mass, why he'd stand

or kneel, but never sit
for services, every part of him
flowing and vigilant.

Coastal, Aberration

The packing shed and fishermen's homes swell
              in the background, cement and metal against gray sky.

Windows and skylights, even a single church cross,
              reach into the clouds. No work crew in sight.

The men inside must be waiting for weather to pass,
or for the day boat to pull in

with bushels of fish to carry in from the dock,
              ice down for the trip to town,

dreaming of it.

In the foreground, three boats have found their final landing tied to
each other against the riprap. One vessel's sound, but broken up along
its gunwale, another with sturdy bow but torn in half behind its steering
wheel, the third just ribs with enough planks to separate it from the dirt.
The ships are bound together like a monument to work done and over,
time passed, never to come around again.

*

Lichen and rust,

        boat ribs crumbling back to ground—

From earth   to axe   to sea   to shore
and dust.

*

Between, rows of fish traps stacked
        against the wind's bite.
Green nets and yards of twine
        readied for a storm.

*

On wing halfway above the horizon, a pelican fights into the wind. Black and white against the gray, the bird's an aberration, wings pulsing, a shift in tone between squall lines. Maybe it's a harbinger. Maybe a scourge. Maybe, more than the traps, it's proof the sea cannot run barren. Life is not decay, not the slow loss of color and grain. The bird will dive into the surf soon enough, scoop up fish for its young, and carry that catch back to its nest to spark a scene more vibrant than shored boats and empty traps. Even in still photos, the narrative must flow.

*

Stones cover the shoreline, underfoot,
        becoming something other
        than what they are,
smaller, more part of the place,
        making the sea grass green.

Fable, *Un Matin*

As soon as the eyes and snout showed up
floating in his cattle pond one morning,
the farmer began to count the stock

roaming his fields. He'd never taken
inventory before, but thought
his numbers smaller than they ought to be.

He set about watching the alligator
swim around his pond that day,
knowing it wouldn't leave as quickly

as it had appeared. He'd told his children
bedtime stories of wise gators
who'd outwitted raccoons and bullfrogs,

read in wildlife books how long
it took for them to grow past fifteen feet,
how gentle and patient they were

courting love, always circling
and waiting, slapping their broad throats
on the water's surface for attention.

But fables could not save his calves
nosing grass at the water's edge,
nor spare the white chickens pecking

head down along the bank. His ledger
was not difficult to balance.
He had no meat to lose heading

towards winter and plenty 12-gauge shells
back at the house, the walk too short
to break much of a sweat.

Lutins

Today, walking the neighborhood,
I ran across a white cat.

It did not stop for me,
but stared me down

as if I'd offended it
somehow.

Cats always worried
my uncle's camp when I was young.

Even though he kept chinchillas
out back, he trusted the cats

to clean the dock
after he'd baited crab traps.

Not the white ones, though.
He ran those off,

said cats without color
were *lutins.* They turned

to goblins in moonlight,
troubled the horses so much

the animals couldn't walk
rice fields in the mornings.

Lutins rode the horses' backs
until dawn, plaited

their tails and manes
to let the farmers know

who owned the fields
first. No keyhole was ever

small enough to keep *lutins* out
if they wanted in.

My uncle always said
he was happy to have

more horses than hair.
Can't say I ever understood that

until now.

Père Papineau

—an Acadian folk tale

I.

The old man should not be met
　　at water's edge.

He will come inland,
　　follow you back home

hungry.

Always leave him to his thoughts,
　　the heron's cry.

II.

Wanderer   no bog or hollow
the old man hasn't crossed.

His hunger pulls him around,
bottomless, ready to consume a man's weight.

Never try to feed his demands
or give him reason to cast spells.

There's not enough rice in the field
nor chickens in the coop

to fill the hole in his gut.
Do not confuse his wanting with need.

III.

The nature of the marsh
is to take things in,
interlace water and reed,
heat and sound,
stranger and friend.

The old man, though,
is dos-gris,
and we are all mullet
in his world.

Raconte

Whenever anything I cared about
    went missing, my mother
        told me the story of bears

who struggled every day
    to find the things
        they needed. They had no home

and moved around without rest
    under moonlight.
        She said they could cover

hundreds of miles before
    sunrise. There was never
        any logic to the things

the bears took, mother told me.
    Even they didn't know
        what sparkly thing,

or noise maker,
    or special picture book
        they had to have

until they held it
    in their huge paws,
        caught its shine in their eyes.

Dead Turtle

My daughter leaves the body
as it lies, will not disturb
the turtle's last stretch
to position it with more grace.

She covers it with azalea petals
to cool its skin, outlines
its body in concentric circles
of branches, swatches
torn from magazines—

there is no other shelter to offer
from the sun or ants, save
color and soft voices.

In some other place, she will find
song to hold all of this, enlaced.

A Wedding, In Rain

It's good luck, the rain, my wife says
to the stranger behind us.

If I was any luckier, the man smiles back,
they'd put me in jail, then.

And the young preacher starts
talking about hard times and how

people are worse more than they are
better. And the young couple

cares nothing about sermons
or luck or how the raindrops

fall straight through the giant oak
reaching out over their heads.

They just hold hands and look
into each other's eyes, see

the person they know is right
there with them, not the flawed

sinner the young preacher keeps
telling them they'll wake up to

tomorrow. And the old people
daubing rain off their glasses

know the walk back up
to the reception hall won't be

nearly as kind, uphill and slick
after this little blessing of luck.

But for right now, there's song
and prayer and promises,

more than two people
happy to be here, wet.

Les Ris

Sweet roll dough,
yellow with yolk,

waits in the warm spot
on top the fridge.
It swells under a kitchen towel,

alive and becoming
the reason Sundays glow,

promises we roll
and cut, bake and glaze,
share with lips already parted,
smiling.

Coda

Afternoons beside the spillway,
old men cast lines into the water

and stare at their corks,
waiting still for the channel cat

that stole their bait decades ago
to pull itself out of the silt,

rise giant and hungry
toward the last hook they have.

Author's Note

Jack B. Bedell is Professor of English and Coordinator of Creative Writing at Southeastern Louisiana University where he also edits *Louisiana Literature* and directs the Louisiana Literature Press. His latest collections are *Elliptic* (Yellow Flag Press, 2016) and *Bone-Hollow, True: New & Selected Poems, Call & Response, Come Rain, Come Shine, What Passes for Love* and *At the Bonehouse*, all published by Texas Review Press (a member of the Texas A&M Press Consortium). His work has appeared in the *Southern Review, Sport Literate, The Fourth River, Hudson Review, Connecticut Review, Paterson Literary Review, Texas Review, Southern Quarterly*, and other journals. Bedell is the recipient of the Louisiana Endowment for the Humanities Individual Achievement in the Humanities Award and the Governor's Award for Artistic Achievement, and he is a three-time finalist or Louisiana Poet Laureate. He and his wife Beth have three children, Jack, Jr., Samuel Eli, and Emma Louise.